Quadrille
PUBLISHING

CONTENTS

Introduction

I believe that decorating can change lives. It can make us happier by raising our spirits the moment we walk through the door, it can relax us, and it can make entertaining and hanging out at home way more fun.

But, and this is a big BUT, if you want life-changing interiors – the ones that make your heart beat just that little bit faster – you need an open mind and a big dose of self-belief.

As we all know, style has absolutely nothing to do with money. I've seen hundreds, no, thousands of tasteful, colour coordinated spaces that are expensively decorated and yet flat, dull, uptight and bland. They don't seduce, tantalise or increase the pulse rate because they have been decorated to within an inch of their lives. What a yawn!

I gravitate towards spaces that mesmerise – that make me want to kick my shoes off and hang out. You know how you feel when you walk into a room with a fire gently burning in the grate, or bread baking in the oven? I want that feeling in each and every interior I design. The best tip I can give you is, don't stop decorating too soon. Most people do. And yet it's the rugs, cushions, cool lighting, texture, pattern, flowers, art and one-off pieces that add layers and dimension to a room. You won't dazzle friends, guests, family or the Joneses with your pad unless you fill it with stuff, and lots of it!

Make it personal

I'm often asked how I came up with my aesthetic and I can honestly say that it simply evolved. I started out painting my house top-to-toe white and favoured a very simplistic, minimal Scandinavian interior. Then I started experimenting. I painted one wall dark and the transformation was so stunning that I immediately crossed over to the dark side and painted the whole interior in inky sludgy hues. I ditched the Scandi look – far too dull with dark walls! – and embraced eclecticism.

As I've grown in confidence, my style has grown with me. It has become somewhat kaleidoscopic, since I pull from so many different periods and sources. Nothing follows a theme – if I respond to a piece emotionally, I buy it.

The trick is to experiment and have fun along the way. So I might hang a neo baroque chandelier over a rustic table, plonk an over-sized 1970s vase on top, finish it off with a few accessories – books, candles, a silver pig. Nothing really matches and yet it all makes perfect sense. I've created magic!

Pushing the boundaries is liberating stuff. It means you end up with a home that is distinctly and beautifully yours.

This book will help you find your own unique sense of style. Forget rules, trends or forecasts. It's about filling your home with stuff you love and find uplifting, and doing it with confidence. Too much tastefulness is dull and too much fun is tacky, it's all about getting the balance right.

Interiors that ooze style are not perfectly coordinated nor can they be bought out of a catalogue. Instead, I will show you how to take rooms to a whole other level with unexpected solutions, savvy styling and inexpensive finds.

It takes time to scavenge flea markets, scour eBay and visit auction houses. And on the DIY side, you will need confidence to start with. But my projects are designed to give you just that.

So whether you fancy crafting a cool letter light out of foam core (page 142), designing your own roller blinds (page 32), or creating a chevron floor (page 96), the steps are super simple, fun and quick to implement.

The more creative you get with decorating, the more addictive it becomes. So what if you don't have the bucks to buy that beautiful vintage Moroccan Berber rug? Paint one on the floor instead... Happy decorating!

Style *guide*

WHAT'S YOUR STYLE?

With all the visual stimuli out there, it's easy to feel overwhelmed. Creating a mood board will give you a clear vision of your style right from the get go. Find inspiration in books, magazines, blogs, and websites (there's a list of my favourites on page 188), and pull out images you are immediately attracted to. Do any similarities shine through? Are you drawn to rooms that are bold and blingy, modern, eccentric or classic? Don't worry if the looks don't match. The more styles you introduce the more intriguing your space will be.

CLASSIC

With a nod to the past and a wink to the future, classic style is all about balance, symmetry and order. It's formal, it's elegant and it's a style that marries luxe materials (think metallics) with super-glam fabrics (think cashmere and leather). Woods are often dark, furniture often crisp and defined; symmetry abounds.

GLAMOROUS

Glamorous interiors are layered, theatrical, elegant and exotic. From daring palettes to tantalising textiles to exaggerated scale you need to be a little fearless with this style. Go bold with colour or add a little sheen through rich metallics – it's all about mixing styles from around the globe. Individuality and imagination are key.

eclectic

A kaleidoscopic blend of pieces make up eclectic interiors, and literally anything goes – from mid-century modern to pop art to a smidge of baroque. It's a hard look to pull off since nothing matches yet it's all got to make perfect sense. A highly creative and innovative style, you bring it together by harmonising and contrasting colour, texture, shape and finish.

BOHO
Boho pads are uninhibited, cosy, cocooning and fabulously idiosyncratic. Comfort is all-important; from deep squishy armchairs to homespun fabrics to the warm hues on the walls. Think rustic and offbeat, with the odd drippy chandelier or jewelled accessory making the whole thing sparkle and shimmer.

ROCK 'N' ROLL

Rock 'n' roll interiors set convention aside and push a few boundaries. This is decorating as self-expression. Think furniture in oddball finishes, daring high voltage jolts of colour, salon style art and playful proportions. It's bold, it's blingy and it's fabulous!

Room Analysis

Walls Feature walls are sneered at by some, but I really love them. This double-height wall covered in bookcase wallpaper has become my favorite hang-out nook.

Style A mix of styles – classic and boho furniture, tribal and zebra print rugs – creates a highly personalised layered look.

Greenery Every interior needs a dash of greenery: foliage and little clusters of flowers elevate a space to new heights.

Scale Vary the height of your furniture and lights. If everything is the same height it's a big yawn – instead, you want to create visual intrigue.

My kind of design flirts with going over the top, but I consciously pull it back from the edge.

CLASSIC

If you're bored of passing fads, classic style never goes out of date. This look can be super traditional or beautifully relaxed, but furniture – formal, elegant, balanced – must stand the test of time.

If your home has any architectural features, cherish them. Curved lines and decorative mouldings work perfectly with this style, so even if you don't live in a period building, think about adding some simple architectural elements of your own. Visit salvage yards for period items, or DIY stores for modern reproductions, which are easy to install and relatively cheap.

A simple moulding like coving, which runs around the top of walls, at the junction with the ceiling, can add a wonderful layer of texture to walls and ceilings Ceiling roses provide a beautiful focal point to a room. Even the humble skirting board can give character to modern boxy rooms.

Looking for an even cheaper option? Paint faux panelling directly onto walls (page 124).

A Classic Hallway
Traditional prints on the wall, a bygone chandelier and an elegant runner. Clean lined, formal and super smart, this is classic decorating at its best!

how to add flair *to your* stairs

A fabulous way to spruce up your hallway is to wallpaper the stair risers. Use leftover paper from a previous project, vintage patterns or buy a one-off extraordinary roll!

1. Measure each rise separately and cut the wallpaper to fit exactly.

2. To prep the stairs, give them a quick once over with warm soapy water.

SHOPPING LIST

- Retractable tape measure
- Scissors or craft knife
- Wallpaper
- Pasting brush
- Wallpaper paste
- Sponge
- Decorator's varnish

3. Apply paste to the back of the wallpaper and adhere each strip, starting in the corner and working across and down with your fingers as you go. Wipe off any paste with a sponge and run a brush over to smooth out bubbles.

4. Once the glue has dried, it's a good idea to apply a special decorator's varnish (for wallpapered surfaces) for added protection against scuffing toes.

Top Tip

Embrace pattern – it will make the risers feel far more intriguing than if you simply opted for a textured paper. And take care to choose a pattern that works within the space of the risers.

Classic Details

Use classic checks, houndstooth, floral prints, pretty birds, geometric pattern or tone on tone colour to add interest. Paul Smith has the most beautiful burnt orange, striped upholstery fabric – traditional, with a twist. And I'm a big fan of Nina Campbell's classic Perroquet wallpaper.

For a quieter vibe, take inspiration from nature and go down the textured route, with soft grass cloth, faux leather wall coverings, even fake wood panelling.

When it comes to colour, experiment with earthy tones (terracotta, taupe and moss). You can go darker (with olive, peat and charcoal) or very light (think linen, lilac and stone), but avoid anything too jarring – a classic room needs to feel warm and inviting. By all means go for striking accents, but opt for darker hues rather than neo brights. Or combine dark wall shades with white woodwork for an iconic look.

Do the Twist Don't follow the rulebook too strictly with this look as things will become predictable and boring. To add an edge, maybe plonk a slogan print in a traditional frame, mismatch the furniture or add tassles to plain door handles.

The Finishing Touches From ornate pineapple sconces and beautiful carved mirrors to iconic Fornasetti plates, classic decorative pieces need to look semi-traditional. Symmetry is key, so look for pairs of lamps, urns, mirrors, vases. Add a little sparkle with chandeliers or wall lights in glass and metallics. Sure we want beautiful, relaxing order, but we also want the jaw on the floor!

how to
create your own
plate art

From granny's posh china to discount dishes snagged at the local charity shop, plates have been adorning walls for years. Recently, however, they seem to be having a moment. Hung higgledy-piggledy in varying sizes, or all the same size and displayed in straight lines, they add a lovely decorative element to alcoves and little nooks. Silhouette art is simple to paint (or copy) and looks fabulously high end, or experiment with your own design.

SHOPPING LIST

- Paper and scissors
- Fine-point permanent marker
- Plain white plates
- Fine-tipped paint brush
- Black ceramic paint
- Plate hangers and picture hooks

1. Draw a silhouette that you like, or if you can't paint, find a silhouette in a book or online and photocopy it.

2. Cut out the silhouette, then trace the image onto the plate using a fine-point permanent marker.

3. Very carefully paint the inside of the silhouette with the black paint, and then fill in the middle.

4. Some ceramic paints require oven-baking to seal in the colour; some don't. Always follow the manufacturer's instructions.

5. When the paint is dry, hang or mount the plate from the wall or rest on a shelf.

Top Tip

Plate hangers can be found at any DIY store. I go for invisible discs where the hook rests at the bottom of the plate – it means your plates will lay flat on the wall as opposed to away from it slightly.

BOHO

I love this style of decorating since there are no rules. Instead, boho is all about experimenting, expressing yourself and being as creative as you like. It's a fabulously fun approach.

To pull the look off, you need a good eye for colour and a big dose of wild abandon. Styles and shapes aren't important – it's all about a mix and match attitude, creating spaces that have a global influence but a casual feel. If you fancy the sound of a rustic flea market chair with a 1950s Hollywood chandelier, this is your look!

Boho interiors ooze personality. Dispensing with formality, they are enchanting spaces where you instantly want to sit down, hang out and fling off your shoes.

Pretty Little Things
Glam up boho interiors with lace, beads, sequins and shells. Sterile white will feel too stark, so layer on the accessories. Cosseting neutrals work beautifully. Ivory, milk and buttery taupe give a cosy comforting feel; organic textures and shapes exude warmth.

Savvy Chic The great thing about boho is that you don't need a big budget. In fact, it helps not to be too precious about what you buy – the coolest boho interiors are filled with stuff gathered from car boot sales and auction houses, alongside well-loved hand-me-downs. Pieces that tell a story are the perfect fit. And the emphasis is on comfort. Look for big squishy sofas, inviting armchairs; coffee tables for putting up feet; occasional tables with a rustic feel.

Top Tip

You can pull anything off with a boho interior: a great big moose head on the wall, cow skin floating across the floor, an assortment of hodge podge art. It's all about creating as many different textures and layers as possible.

Boho Colours

Boho walls can be painted in any hue. Hardcore bohemians go opposite ends of the spectrum, partnering red with green, or orange with purple, for a confident hippy vibe. You can opt for soft neutrals, or warm things up with aged natural wood, or old tin tiles that have a beautiful patina.

Earthy hues work wondrously with vintage accessories; a mix of jewelled and metallic colours add something new again. Get loud and busy with stars and stripes, squiggles, diamonds or flowers. Or mix a zillion different patterns together. Create balance in the room by reining in the colour palette.

Next, pile on the accessories. The more layers you add, the more exciting a space becomes. Collect flea market art, mismatched vases, interesting lampshades; save quirky postcards and souvenirs. You want it to look like you've travelled all over the world – even if you haven't!

Lush Bedding More interchangeable than furniture, plus you can switch it up with the seasons. Figuring out your bedding first will help you set the mood. With my bedroom (see below) I already had the slubby woollen throw, which set the boho tone, so I just worked from there, adding a textural panelled wall, and a chandelier crafted from mud. LOVE!

Insouciant Glamour
Just because boho tends to be rustic and offbeat doesn't mean it can't be glamorous. Drippy chandeliers and ornate gold mirrors fit into this style just fine. The thing is to have fun with your designs; unexpectedness is key to a fabulous interior.

Glamorous

There is a reason why glamorous interiors have enjoyed unparalleled popularity from the elegance of Art Deco to the Hollywood Regency era to the modern day. It is that this style is utterly flattering: elegant, sophisticated, sexy and lavish. This is the decorating equivalent of putting on a little black dress: suddenly everything feels and looks super chic!

You want to conjure up the appearance of luxury – expensive fabrics, opulent furnishings, bespoke lighting and a sense of sumptuousness. But the glamorous look doesn't have to cost big bucks. Embellish existing pieces, be creative and discover your sense of drama.

Flea markets have the coolest selection of vintage fabrics – velvet, fur, silk, leather and animal prints. And high street buys can be embellished with a little braiding, fringing or feathers. When it comes to furnishings, opt for pieces with a more formal structure. Glossy touches – like an ornate gold candelabra on a little rustic table – add a feeling of casual grandeur.

A High Voltage Jolt
A punch of colour can make your interior feel super glam. Add a striking piece of furniture, like this red leather vintage chair, which I adore!

Supersize Play around with scale, light and a seductive inky colour palette to amp up the intrigue a notch.

how to revamp *your* rollers

SHOPPING LIST

- Protective sheets
- Roller blind
- Wallpaper
- Retractable tape measure
- Scalpel
- Wallpaper paste
- Pasting brush and paint brush

Smart, tailored and utterly simple, roller blinds are the perfect shade for small windows. To transform a bland, boring roller into something you might find in a boutique hotel, wallpaper it. You can go big and bold with pattern, as the area you are covering is so compact. If you can afford it, opt for wallpaper that has been hand blocked (rather than machine produced); the colour has way more depth, and the effect is utterly tantalising. Since you only need a remnant, it won't cost the earth. Check that the colours and print you select are in harmony with the rest of the room.

1. Cover the area you're working on with protective sheets.

2. Roll out the blind to its full length and cut the wallpaper to fit exactly. Aim for a perfect fit as it is messy to start trimming paper once the gluing is done.

3. Using a clean brush, apply paste to the back of the wallpaper. Work from one end of the wallpaper to the other, starting off in the corner.

4. Lay the roller blind on a flat surface (I use the floor) and apply the wallpaper to it, working from one end to the other and smoothing out any bubbles as you go with a brush.

5. Let the paste dry, then install your shade.

Top Tip

Select wallpaper that is roughly the same thickness as the blind. Anything too thin will need to be lined first.

Lights and Colour

There are plenty of ways to add razzle dazzle to a room. You can up the glam ratings by embracing gloss and all things lacquered and shiny. I'm the hugest fan of spraying flea market finds in the brightest hues possible, to add colour and a hint of drama.

Adopt a black and white + one accent colour scheme, or be as inventive, unexpected and dramatic as you like: deep fuchsia with grey; shimmery gold walls with yellow accents. Nuts possibly, but glamorous interiors can handle the dramatic!

To finish off the look, good lighting is essential. Little pools of soft light create the most seductive ambience. Chandeliers will give your space a bit of Tinseltown glitz and are even more dramatic if you use them in unexpected areas like kitchens, landings and bathrooms.

The absolute best thing of all when it comes to upping the glam ratings is a dimmer: lighting can change the mood of a room in an instant, and once you've tried dimmers you will never switch back!

Top Tip

Something I do time and time again is supersize the mirrors in the bathrooms I design. This is done with great effect here. Firstly it makes the bathroom look and feel lavish and sophisticated; secondly, if your space is bijou like this, it adds a magical allure that a standard mirror just wouldn't do.

Sparkle and Shine

Mirrors reflect light, add depth, expand horizons and add a feeling of enchantment. To ramp up the bling, accessorise with lustrous metallics that reflect the light and make everything shine and shimmer.

eclectic

Eclectic interiors marry multiple ideas, a medley of styles and diverse sources to create a look that screams one-of-a-kind. Scary stuff? You bet! But, for me, it's the coolest look around. In fact, interiors that are the most memorable to my mind draw from a plethora of references, from granny to cowboy.

The eclectic look requires creativity and innovation, and since it's characterised by a freedom of expression, there's a danger it can descend into chaos. But if you combine a spirit of adventure with some basic principles of design, it is possible to bring uniformity to any given scheme and pull the whole thing off.

My first tip would be to think carefully about colour. The only rule when it comes to creating eclectic interiors is that they look consistent and harmonious. By all means clash colours, but it helps to stick to a restricted number of hues in order to tie all the elements together (page 86).

I'm at my happiest when mixing the rustic unfinished natural look with accessories that are slicker, grander and a little more glam. I decorate with dark inky sludgy hues and then accent with the odd bright punch; the rest of my accessories and furnishings are kept neutral.

So long as you rein in the colour scheme, you can mix and match to your heart's content. Push boundaries by playing around with matt and shiny finishes. Go big on multiple fabrics: textured, patterned or a combination of the two. Team geometrics with muted colours, plaids with stripes. Mix styles, eras and influences – it makes things way more exciting!

Some Like it Hot

Homes are reflecting our personalities like never before. This kind of decorating takes confidence, but if you can put seemingly disparate objects together in a room and allow them to simmer, the temperature will rise! Designing this way is incredibly addictive. And just to warn you, you're never done!

Going the Extra Mile Every room needs a focal point (or two, or three) to draw the eye and pull a scheme together. If you don't have something grounding like a fireplace or a large window, decide what this might be. Salon style art on a wall works brilliantly, as does a great bunch of blooms; artfully dressed shelves; a rug or an oddball chair.

Make it Pretty The eclectic look is one of the hardest to pull off. And yes, I've made mistakes. I've brought furniture from far-flung places that looked great in the souk only to get home and find the piece doesn't work in one single room, even the garden (believe me I tried)! Mistakes are all part and parcel of the process – you won't get to create exciting, enchanting, idiosyncratic interiors unless you take a few risks.

Something Unexpected You can create harmony and cohesion through form, Here, the dog light and sculpture hanging out together on a console doesn't feel crazy as the similarity in form unifies the scheme. Houseplants, supersized or otherwise, introduce a fab burst of colour and wake up a room beautifully.

ROCK 'N' ROLL

If you like your bad boy bling, this is the look to roll with. Rock 'n' roll decorating is flamboyant, sophisticated, a little saucy, carried off with a huge dose of confidence. Think animal print rugs, gold accessories, graphic cushions, some super cool graffiti wallpaper – all statement-worthy stuff!

The trick is to scale down the tack and up the luxury vibe. It helps to identify a few anchors. For me, a rock 'n' roll interior usually starts with colour, followed by either a large piece of furniture or artwork, or maybe an amazing rug. Playing around with scale is a vital part of the magic. Plonk over-sized lamps on teeny tiny tables, or suspend chandeliers that are too big on ceilings that are too low.

Push the colour palette. You want to go as non-traditional as possible, so think black instead of white, cobalt, crimson and other high voltage hues. No colours are off limits – this is bad boy decorating after all, so you can do as you darn well please!

Overdose on shine; from mirrored occasional tables to metallic wallpaper to lacquered coffee tables and chairs, glossy, reflective surfaces add instant glamour.

Top Tip

The biggest tip I can give you would be to start small. Decorating a bijou area like a hallway or the bathroom will build your confidence, particularly if this is a look you haven't embraced before.

Rock Furnishings

Select standalone pieces that add drama – a patent leather sofa, a massive gold chandelier – 'conversation starters', as they're known in the biz. Gravitate to strong rather than delicate, masculine rather than frou-frou pieces – they're a lot hipper.

Every rock 'n' roll interior needs some cool art, so display the stuff you love, or take inspiration from Banksy and graffiti over cheap flea market art (page 119).

Once you've got the basics covered, go as funky as you want with the accessories. It's all about expressing yourself and having no limits. This is your opportunity to go nuts!

Visual Friction All this stuff shouldn't work together, but by making sure the key pieces relate in some way – through colour, style or period – you end up with polished cool as opposed to a wannabe mess. Here the big statement rug unites the rest of the scheme through colour. Even less obvious hues are cleverly mirrored elsewhere in the space.

Space
Matters

The nature of your space will inevitably push your design in certain directions, but whether you live in a shoebox in the city or a sprawling farmhouse, the trick is to utilise to the max. By which I mean embracing every single nook and cranny!

In overcrowded cities like NYC, London and Paris, I've seen some ingenious use of small spaces: passageways and hallways double dutying as home offices; desks, wardrobes, even bedrooms carved out of alcoves.

You may not be able to change the physical dimensions of your space, but you can absolutely change the perception of its size. You can add visual interest through dazzling colour, luxe fabrics or a playful use of scale. You can think vertically (by installing high-up shelving, for example). A decorative screen, even a large plant, can help zone off areas, creating stylish dual function rooms, full of those all-important layers I like to bang on about.

Getting the furniture placement right is absolutely essential for happy decorating. If all your stuff happens to be up one end, it can make a room feel unbalanced. If furniture is plonked too close to walls, your space will look uptight and dull.

What we are after are pads that are squishy and comfortable, beautiful yet functional, with an assortment of furnishings that have been both obviously arranged and surprisingly so. Here's how to do it...

Open Plan Rooms

Open plan living is all the rage – rooms that spill into each other, kitchens into dining rooms, bathrooms into bedrooms. These over-sized spaces can look fab and have obvious benefits – the ability to hang out with guests while cooking, or to keep an eye on the dogs while working! But with few walls, tons of floor space and a larger area to fill, they are tricky to get right.

I find it far easier to design open plan rooms if I imagine the walls back in place. Firstly this helps when figuring out traffic flow, and secondly it gives each room its own sense of purpose.

It also helps to assess practicalities. For instance, is the dining area located close to the kitchen? You don't want to be transporting hot food halfway through the zone! Consider noise: is the washing machine going to drown out the sound of the TV? Think about views: do you want the sofa overlooking the garden or the dining room? The earlier all of this stuff gets figured out the better.

With open plan spaces suitably divided, create a sense of connection through a consistent colour palette on walls and ceilings. And stick with one style of flooring throughout – you don't want a space broken up with lots of different treatments.

I've got concrete throughout my lower ground floor, but then I've layered and skimmed rugs over rugs to create focal points. The principle is the same for colour too; with the background hues providing calm, you can add distinct pops of pattern, colour and texture to define separate areas.

Add Depth The best interiors challenge you to inspect, wonder and touch, so there is an aura of adventure and discovery. A space falls flat if furniture is just plonked flat against walls. Look at your space as you would a forest. In my interiors, paths are never straight; you have to meander and set your own course.

Zoning In

Design your lighting so that it visually separates each zone – this is pretty fundamental and yet lighting is often neglected, or treated as an afterthought.

In our house, I've got downlighters in the kitchen and the dining room, with a beaded chandelier hanging low over the central island for an unexpected twist. All of the downlights are dimmable, so I can create and adjust a mood instantly. In the dining and living areas, I've swapped to a far more intimate arrangement: lamps on tables and lamps on the floor.

Give neglected areas an instant facelift with a chair or maybe an occasional table, or create a cool bar out of any old table to enliven the kitchen, dining or living areas. Add warmth through little details – candles, lamps, blooms, sweet ceramic bowls – and you've pretty much nailed it.

So maybe your open plan space lacked cosiness and intimacy before, but not any more right?

Divide and Conquer

The trick with open plan spaces is to divide the room into different zones that are independent in look and feel, yet harmonise with the overall scheme. This pad pretty much nails it – the lounging zone feels clubby and library-esq; the dining area is more rustic; the space is united by a colour palette that is beautiful and cohesive.

Terrific Texture

A great way of cosying up open plan spaces is texturising. The floors in this loft are concrete yet they don't feel harsh or cold as the area is layered with rugs, throws, wood and glass. The more texture you add the more intrigue you add!

Small is Beautiful

Small rooms are my idea of heaven. I love how cosy they are. In fact, whenever I get to work on large spaces I always zone them off to create lots of little vignettes or living areas.

If you want a small room to work, embrace the snugness and ditch conventional rules like choosing small-scale furniture or painting rooms in pale hues. Nothing gets my blood pressure zooming into the stratosphere more than the misconception that pale colours open up a room. A small room is a small room. Painting it pale is not going to double its size or even make it look marginally bigger!

Chuck out what you don't need. If you add wardrobes, take them to the ceiling for a streamlined effect. (This is great, as you get to store more stuff!) The trick, the biggest single most important thing you can do, is to paint everything in the same hue. I'm talking ceilings, walls, woodwork and trim – floors too, if you dare – so it looks like you've just dipped the whole room into a bucket of paint. Not only will this make a space feel more cohesive, it takes away boundaries and you're left with infinity. Plus, everything you place in the room will look amazing. Promise!

Dazzle It's not about maintaining a sense of spaciousness; it's actually about dazzling the eye so it doesn't clock instantly how small the space is. Rather it clocks how cool the place is.

Dress to Impress
Frou-frou up small spaces by giving them a luxe vibe like this bedroom. Full length curtains, sumptuous textiles skimming the bed, a cool sculpture on the wall. It's called kitting out your pad with panache!

Less is a Bore

Don't, I repeat, don't downsize the furniture to 'fit' the room. In order for a space to look magical you've got to mess around with scale. Supersized pieces can add instant grandeur.

The trick is to vary the height of your furniture, accessories and lighting to create a lively rhythm. If you opt for everything the same height, and the same size, your interiors are going to have that classic ailment known as 'drab room syndrome'.

Pattern has the potential to make a room appear smaller or larger, so experiment with vertical stripes on walls (page 94). Make sure the area is evenly lit: lots of small pools of light to draw the eye. Oh and ditch the old mantra that less is better for small spaces. Mumbo jumbo!

Pack a Punch Rather than sporting a conservative minimal look, the homeowner has embraced the room's smallness and decorated with attitude – tons of pictures on walls, cushions on sofas, piles of books and rugs skimming rugs.

The Smallest Room in the House

Designing a bathroom is a matter of mixing function and practicality with style and maybe a soupçon of glamour. Oftentimes we neglect the latter. Time and money are spent on fixtures and hardware, yet somehow we forget to personalise the look.

No matter its size, your bathroom can feel grown up and glam; somewhere you want to hang out and spend time. The key is to start thinking about accessories.

Vintage mirrors are very Hollywood-esq, candles add intrigue, a sweet stool or little impromptu chair will add comfort. Mix in some flowers or plants and finally plonk a bath tap over the sink for Alice in Wonderland grandeur. Suddenly your bathroom looks like something in the pages of a cool magazine. Easy, no?

Decorate Unconventionally Who cares if the room is only big enough to house a shower? Push the colour envelope!

Accessorise Dress up your bathroom with art, postcards or letters; they soften a stark space and add a fresh and delightful dimension at the same time as injecting instant personality.

Dual Function Rooms

Not everyone has the space to devote a whole room to a certain function, and city dwellers in particular have to be ingenious at utilising every single nook of a place.

Forget convention; think out of the box and glamorise. If you only have space for a bijou dining table in the kitchen make sure it looks pretty darn cool. Invest in some stylish multi-purpose furniture: coffee tables that double as storage chests, sofa beds, stools with lids, nests of tables – that sort of thing.

Let's take a space that double duties as a bedroom and office. Ditch anything purely practical and corporate looking. Instead, opt for a console or dining table in a zingy colour rather than the traditional office desk. Jazz up the lighting, introduce rugs, flowers, candles and accessories so that the office area blends seamlessly with the rest of the bedroom.

It's all about seducing the eye with surface attractions. Done well, your dual-function rooms can feel every bit as beautiful as the rest of your home!

Dressy Details Cool little touches like papering your kitchen with boho wallpaper, or suspending a beaded chandelier over a table, take a utilitarian multi-functional space to a whole other level. It takes the emphasis away from boring practicalities and onto the glamorous, the beautiful and the "Ta Da!"

Room Analysis

Display Floor to ceiling bookcases don't feel cluttered as they are broken up with some front-facing tomes, objects, little cards and letters.

Lighting An assortment of quirky lights and a playful sense of scale really ups the interest.

Double Duty When it comes to home offices, choose a table that doesn't look corporate. Mine is a vintage dining table, which I've spray painted a beautiful teal.

To get jaw on the floor fabulous interiors, you need to go a little off radar!

Furniture Move furniture away from the perimeter and angle it slightly to break up the boxiness of a room.

Furniture Placement

One of the easiest ways to re-energise a room is to rearrange the furniture. It can feel daunting trying to figure out how to do this, but when you break it down, furniture placement is all about creating harmony and balance.

The biggest no no, which I see time and time again, is furniture shoved against walls. I'm guessing people do this because they think rooms will look bigger with the furniture skimming the perimeter. WRONG! They will look and feel as boring as the layout.

Bring sofas into the centre of a room or, if that scares you, consider placing furniture at an angle, or place a console or skinny piece of furniture behind a sofa to break up the boxiness of a room. As if by magic, your space feels instantly more cocooning and interesting.

In my interiors, paths are never straight. By this I mean that you can't walk in a straight line from one end of the room to the other – you kind of have to chart your own course. Sounds kooky? Bear with me. Consciously (or perhaps subconsciously) you will be more stimulated with this arrangement because it's exciting. You can't clock everything at once and a sense of adventure sets in!

It's practical too, with chairs clustered around fireplaces, sofas sitting at an appropriate distance from the TV. Placing seating around a central table invites conversation.

"The biggest tip I can give you is to move your furniture away from walls, no matter how small your space."

Layers upon Layers

First impressions count. In order to create a warm welcoming ambience, a room must have layers. Any big items, like beds or dining tables, should be broken up with smaller stuff. Layer walls with paintings, beds with throws and pillows, tables with candelabras and flowers. Make sure furniture and accessories feel balanced. Some people go for symmetry here. I tend to go for asymmetry; it adds a slightly more interesting vibe.

Another thing: the more circles you can introduce, the better. Circles break up the boxiness of a space, and add tons of interest. Accessorise with curvaceous lamps and vases, little circular tables and mirrors. The mingling of shapes will instantly break up a room's formality.

Now you just need to add something goofy or a bit whimsical and you've immediately lightened the mood, injected some spirit and turned into an A-list decorator all at the same time!

Distract the Eye TVs are darn right ugly, so take the emphasis away from the black box by layering around it. Think pictures on walls, accessories on shelves. Before long, your TV will look like part of the overall installation and not stand out like a sore thumb.

Inject Character Add flowers, candles. cushions and books – the more layers you pile on, the better. Accessories shake up the monotony of a room and add theatricality. You may not be an exhibitionist but your accessories should be!

Colour, pattern
and texture

I'm a big believer that our homes should reflect our selves – who we are and what we love. To put your individual stamp on a space, the three big hitters are colour, pattern and texture. They're like the herbs and spices of the decorating world, transforming a room from bland to brilliant.

I'm obsessed with colour. It's simple and inexpensive. It takes a room from drab to fab in an instant. It inspires me, but at the same time, it keeps me on my toes. Just when I think I've got the hang of it – wham bam – it disappoints or goes wrong! The key is not to let the mistakes put you off. Learn from them.

I am a huge believer that you have to fail in order to succeed. And ever since I started experimenting with paint I've had this uncontrollable urge to combine colours in new and surprising ways. I have a colour craving addiction, you could say, and one that doesn't seem to be going away!

For a truly tantalising space, texture comes next. Imagine thick velvety curtains beside a small natural bench with a rush seat, or a silk cushion on an old battered leather chair. Consider a variety of materials – a brick wall, a zinc coffee table, glossy painted floors. You can add as much visual variation as you like through texture without your space looking crazy. Overdose on it, I say!

Now throw in some pattern (stripes, abstract, toile, whatever it is that you love) and your space will come alive. If you restrict the colour palette, you can deploy as many patterns as you please.

Years of working in this business have taught me one thing: the memorable rooms are the ones that look genuinely different, and this cannot be achieved without embracing colour, pattern and texture to the max!

Enhancing Neutrals

I have a confession to make; in the past I've been a little down on neutral colour schemes. I guess it comes from seeing one space too many with walls and floors all decorated and coordinated in the same subdued hues. Super drab!

Neutrals fall into two categories: warm – think taupe, putty, brown and cream. And cool – think grey, blue, stone and white. So far, so far from spectacular. To take the look up a notch, the trick is to mix the palette with some high voltage jolts – contrast electric blue with, say, taupe; neon lime green with grey; fluro pink with white.

Ramp up the interest through shape and texture too. The furniture you choose can have a huge impact, so partner a retro coffee table with a traditional chesterfield-type sofa. Marry a chunky wingback chair with a delicate curvaceous side table. Mix masculine and feminine: graceful and decorative with minimal and sleek.

Experiment If you're nervous about making too bold a statement, introduce colour in small ways. Start with an odd wall, an alcove or a transitional area that you are not going to spend a lot of time in. Once you know what you like, push it further, be brave; experiment!

Colour Pops When you enhance neutrals with some oddball shots of colour, the results can be truly electrifying.

Top Tip

Mix multiple styles; the more layers of texture and colour you add, the more interesting and spontaneous a space becomes. Details bring a space alive; they add luxury, warmth and are a room's ultimate indulgence!

Don't Play it Safe

Too much tastefulness is dull. Harmoniously hued rooms need an off note. If you're opting for a neutral palette, create interest through shape and texture. An interplay of different fabrics and surfaces can breathe life into neutral rooms, so cover sofas with throws and cushions; partner silk with velvet, tweed with cotton, faux fur with wool. Pay a lot of attention to styling.

I bang on about this a lot, but as much visual contrast as possible is the trick. Smooth, rough, matte, glossy, hard, soft – there is no limit to your choices! If you've gone super pale on the walls then opt for accessories in deeper darker shades – it will make your room feel far cosier.

Enhancing neutrals with some serious shots of colour is totally transformative; they feel unpredictable, edgy and unexpected. Whoever thought I'd be saying that about neutrals!

All the Beige Vary the tonality of the colours, and use different shapes to create interest in rooms decorated in neutral hues.

High Contrast Push the colour palette with your accent hues. This sideboard literally pops out from the wall thanks to that dark background. Tres chic!

Colour Combining

Selecting the right colour palette for your home is probably the single most important decision you will make as a decorator. A can of paint has incredible impact, whether that's a whole room painted out in zingy red, or a tiny teeny bit of wall painted black. But with thousands of colour choices out there, choosing the right hue is a daunting task.

You can study the colour spectrum and you can learn about complementary contrasting and harmonious colours, and primary, secondary and tertiary colours (bored yet?) Or you can take my advice and ignore all that!

The thing I hate about rules is that they make us less creative. So if I may, let me suggest that you look at colour on an instinctive level.

How does it make you feel?

As abstract as it may seem at first, the initial stage in developing a colour palette for your home is to see the colours around you. Colour is personal and it's all about taking a journey of discovery. Take your time, keep an open mind and don't be swayed by passing trends.

Some tips
Whenever I have a colour conundrum I do the following:

- I look for inspiration everywhere, from nature to the sky to the city.

- I trawl my wardrobe and look at my clothing choices as it gives me an instant starting point for my palette, which I then tweak and twist.

- I list all the colours that I know I love.

- I revisit the colours that I hate and try and figure out why. The more narrow minded and shut down you are about colour combos the more boring your scheme will be. Promise!

Dazzle A can of paint in a rock 'n' roll colour like red can transform mundane rooms into magical ones! Take it one step further and go glossy (as here) and you will add an entirely new dimension and depth to your interior. Red stimulates, it makes us feel happier, so it's a fabulous hue to use in dining and living rooms as well as hallways. It's high impact stuff but the results are dazzling.

Four is the Magic Number

There is no wrong or right when it comes to combining colours. My only advice would be to restrict the number of key colours in a room. I stick to around four – any more and the colours tend to cancel each other out and the room loses impact.

High Voltage Tones

If your home needs a pick-me-up, high voltage tones like magenta, electric blue, saffron and burnt orange will add instant warmth and glamour to a room, no matter the size. I'm never brave enough to use these colours on mass, but I love to accessorise with them as an accent. Dare to go big – with furniture or walls – and you will take your space to a whole other level. Pages 35, 79, 81, 84 and 98 illustrate this point.

Dark Inky Tones

For me, dark inky tones add mystery to a space, a sense of intimacy, edge and glamour. Farrow & Ball's 'Down Pipe' and 'Railings' are my staples. They wrap me up in a thick velvety cloak and give me a deep sense of comfort. Ceilings, floors, walls and trim all get painted out in charcoals, chocolates, deep olives and midnight blues. Accentuate with bold pops of colour, to avoid it feeling depressing and gloomy. Pages 16, 29, 30, 43 and 50 illustrate this point.

Neutral Tones

Easy to live with, timeless, relaxed and laid-back neutral tones are restful and unobtrusive. Although I'm not the greatest fan of neutral colours on walls, I do adore them as an accent, so I've got big squishy caramel velvet sofas, white retro dining chairs, pale, worn away, sandy rugs and straw coloured log baskets. These are comforting hues and essential for any scheme. Pages 18, 28, 39, 41 and 120 illustrate this point.

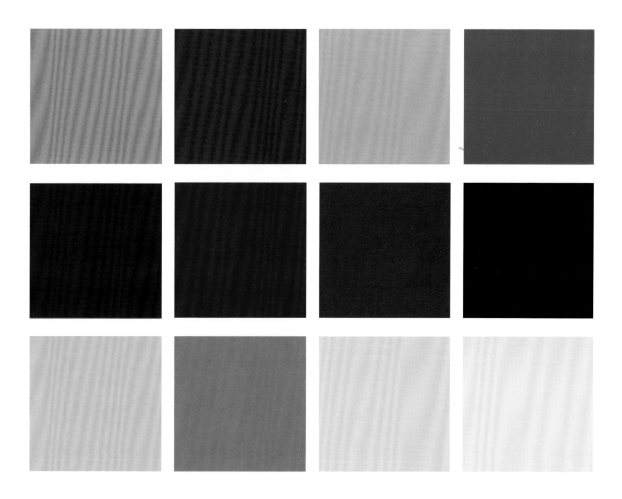

The 1990
LOOSE LIVER
Alternative
CALENDAR
done by children in aid of
SAVE THE CHILDREN
ON SALE HERE

Throw Out the Rulebook

Whether you go dark and inky, bold and clashy, or pale and neutral, I reckon the key to turning a colour scheme into something phenomenal is to push it slightly And the only way to do this is by considering hues that you might normally disregard.

You will make mistakes. I have and I still do, but then you get better at combining. Five years ago, if you told me I would be partnering burnt orange with zingy lime I would have laughed out loud. But that's the great thing about colour, your confidence grows the more you experiment.

Do as I do and paint everything out in one hue. Removing all the visual junctions makes rooms appear bigger and far more sophisticated Alternatively, colour block walls, creating visual interest and impact. Or if you're nervous about making too bold a statement, introduce colour in small ways. Start with a flash of colour in an alcove or a transitional area that you are not going to spend a lot of time in. If you like the results, just keep going!

Colour Uplifts There's no better example of the uplifting effect of colour than in this bijou bathroom. The jolt of striking red paint brings the space alive. The clever part is that it's been used in isolation, so it doesn't overwhelm, instead it tantalises.

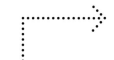

Colour Combos Don't just paint a wall one colour, go graphic with an unexpected combo. This living room wall ups the anty again by adding a contrasting border. It feels fresh and very different.

Pattern Partners

You can have the most beautiful décor around, but if everything in a room strikes the same visual tone, the whole scheme can fall flat. Patterns spice things up a treat.

The plan is to use more than one in a room. Opt for a restricted colour palette so that you have common shades running throughout the scheme. Do that and you can combine a floral pattern with a check, vertical with geometric, paisley with square, and so on.

Patterns are mood-altering, so think about the kind of vibe you want before combining prints. Varying the size and scale of your pattern will give you some beautiful combinations as you crank up the visual intrigue. It's fun to play around with proportions too, so I'll skim the floor of a tiny room with a large print rug, or layer delicate bijou prints in over-sized spaces.

Take the pattern plunge and it's a bit like suddenly discovering you like oysters. You'll be like, why didn't we become buddies before?

Start Small A striking print or patterned table lamps will add interest to any space. Patterned wallpaper makes a big statement. Start small, gain confidence and you can take things to a whole other level.

Shape Up

Believe it or not, you can actually change the perceived shape and size of a room through pattern. If your room is narrow and long, opt for bright patterns that pop – it will immediately make the space feel squarer. If you happen to have low ceilings, consider vertical stripes on walls – ceilings will appear taller than they really are. Conversely, if your ceiling is too high, go for horizontal stripes: it lowers them. See why it's so addictive?

Ceilings If your ceiling lacks any architectural interest, or you want to introduce an arty vibe, get creative with paint. A simple black border adds instant glamour, quirkiness and zing, pushing the eye upwards and transforming the humblest of surfaces.

Floors There is something rather rock star about a harlequin painted floor. It's a decadent treatment so the trick (as we see here) is to partner your diamonds with some seriously glam furnishings and finishing touches. It's a great treatment for small linear rooms like this one, as it takes the focus off the proportions and onto the floor itself.

how to *create a* chevron floor

Designers and A-listers alike adore zigzag rugs as they ooze glamour. Painting yours directly onto the floor makes a super cool statement without costing loads of money!

1. It's vital that the floor is clean before painting begins, so sand the boards down, vacuum, sugar soap and wipe clean of debris with a lint-free cloth and white spirit (pages 181–3). Repeat this process at every stage.

2. Mask off skirting boards and doorframes. Apply primer and undercoat to the floor (the more layers, the better) and allow each application sufficient time to dry.

3. Paint the floor the lighter of the two colours you have picked out. Remember to start painting at the further point from the door to allow yourself an easy exit.

4. When the paint is dry, figure out how many zigs and zags you'd like and the thickness of each stripe. My stripes are each 20cm wide. For the most striking effect, make sure the width of the dark and light stripes is uniform.

5. Measure 20cm (or whatever thickness you prefer) from the bottom of the workspace to the bottom of your first stripe. Pencil in the bottom line of your first 'zig'. Measure 20cm up again and then mark the top line of your zig. Continue in this manner until you have a series of evenly spaced zigzag lines across your surface.

6. Using the masking tape, mark the outside lines of the areas to be darkened. Press the tape down firmly so the paint won't bleed beneath it or curl up on the edges.

7. Apply two or three coats of the darker colour in the direction of the chevron, rather than the direction of the floorboards. As soon as the paint is dry, remove the tape in the direction of the colour – don't let it sit too long or it will stick to the floor. If necessary, touch up the corners with a small paint brush.

SHOPPING LIST
- Sand paper
- Sugar soap
- White spirit
- Masking tape
- Paint brushes
- Primer
- Undercoat
- Two different paint colours
- Pencil and long ruler

Top Tip

This type of flooring is all about contrast, but if you don't fancy the classic combo, keep the white stripes, and substitute black for something zingy and high voltage, like lime green, burnt orange or magenta – great if you fancy a more playful vibe.

Picking Patterns

Cool interiors are those that are genuinely different, so go a little off radar with your patterns for maximum style kudos. By all means opt for gorgeous and perfectly coordinated, but mix in something a little oddball and initially wrong. Consider, for example, a rug with a goofy or kitsch pattern, or maybe go a little crazy in the colour department: yellow mosaic bathroom tiles anyone? Decorating should be a fun process and rooms should reflect that with an element of the unexpected.

A Surprising Hue
It's one of the most underused colours in decorating, and yet look how yellow, used as an anchor colour, enlivens this New York apartment.
It works particularly well when used in unexpected materials, like the ceramic base of this supersized table lamp, for example.

Add Some Quirk Mosaic tiles are the ultimate chic way of adding grandeur to your space. The unusual choice of harvest corn yellow takes it to a different level. Not for the faint-hearted!

Texturising

Overdose on texture, using as many different combinations as you like. The aim here is to create as much friction as possible. Not good in relationships, but a must in interiors!

By texturising, I don't just mean slinging a few cushions on a sofa. I'm thinking light and colour, wallpaper and flooring, hard surfaces and soft furnishings – the more you mix, the more exciting your space will become.

It's the interplay of different fabrics that creates intrigue. Partner silk with wool, velvet with raffia, cotton with sateen. Hard textures require the same attention: for example, you don't want every single chair in the room to be crafted from the same wood. You want some light, some dark, some rough, some smooth, some unfinished, some painted.

Be as bold or as subtle as you want. You can add texture in so many ways: layer your lighting (page 148); ramp up tonal colour variations; or experiment with paint finishes – a glossy ceiling perhaps (amazing when the light hits, bounces and shimmers off), matte walls, an eggshell trim – it all adds a texturised feel to your room.

A Powerful Tool Go for textures that delight your senses, as this will determine not only how a room looks but how it feels as well. With my pad (right), adding a bit of texture transformed my linger time. Before the throws and rugs went down I was in and out in a jiffy. Not so for this bedroom (left). One look at those feathery cushions piled on the bed and I would never want to leave!

Texture Brick walls are the business: whether left untouched or painted, they add a beautiful textural element to a space.

Pattern A wall panel crafted from variegated planks of wood creates a subtle effect that utterly transforms this bedroom.

Colour The zing of green from a grannyish bedspread sets off an interior pulsing with style.

Light Natural light adds another dimension. If you're lucky enough to have big windows don't cover them up!

Ditch convention. Unique touches that reflect your diverse tastes make an interior stand out.

Room Analysis

A Bit of Rough There is nothing so interesting when it comes to texture as juxtaposing something fancy and frou-frou, like this lace curtain, with harsher cold surfaces like brick and concrete. It's all about the contrast; mixing the rough with the refined for a lust-worthy look.

Surface Appeal

The surfaces that frame a room – the walls, floor and ceiling – can transform the mood of your interior dramatically. Hard surfaces (stone, steel, brick, metal, concrete) come alive when juxtaposed with sumptuous textures like cashmere and velvet.

Textured paint is great for adding interest on walls or ceilings (page 116). Cool wallpaper adds instant texture and drama. My latest crush is a paper that emulates vintage tin tiles. I've seen it used in buildings in NYC and am planning on using it as a back splash, on the ceiling, in the loo, anywhere I can! There are so many amazing materials out there – wallpaper that replicates wooden panelling; grass cloth; brick tiles; concrete; tinted plastic; faded leather – all beautiful, beautiful textural finishes. So don't be afraid to experiment with your scheme.

Maximum Effect
A fur stool, a large oil painting, interesting looking tomes, a grandma style rug – these are strange bedfellows indeed! The trick is to restrict the main pattern to one area – the rug (right) – that everything else just feeds off.

how to *make your* *own* vintage light

SHOPPING LIST
- Metal jelly mould
- Hole saw drill cutter
- Pre-wired chrome lamp holder with a bayonet cap (BC)
- Bayonet bulb
- Connector flex

This vintage jelly mould light is quick to make and will add a touch of whimsy to the kitchen, or any room you fancy. Hunt down old tin jelly moulds on eBay, second-hand shops and flea markets. And don't be put off by gentle wear and tear, or any imperfections to the patina – it just adds to the overall beauty.

1. Place the jelly mould upside down on a firm surface and drill a hole slightly bigger than the size of the lamp holder to enable the lamp fixture to be inserted.

2. Insert the base of the lamp fixture into the newly drilled hole and tighten. Follow the installation instructions that come with your light fixture. As with any electrical installation, if in any doubt, consult a qualified electrician.

Top Tip
Buy silk braided flex – it looks far more beautiful than the standard PVC-coated stuff.

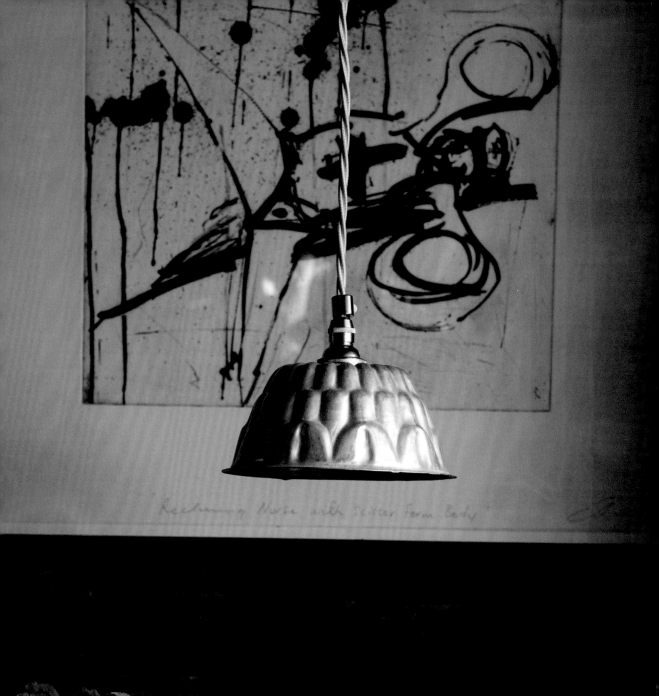

Raising *the bar*

Style has absolutely nothing to do with money. In fact I am often at my most creative when budgets are restricted. The trick is to do things a little differently. Transform rooms with cheap paint or fab accessories. Rethink, reupholster, revamp!

I'm a canny shopper. I try to avoid going down the mass market route and when I do I always embellish to make my purchase feel unique. The secret is to go for something with an attractive structure. If you're buying vintage, don't worry about the state it's in. That's the easiest thing in the world to change (page 129).

Clutter devalues a space. Clever storage works wonders. Shelves and bookcases can be works of art in their own right. Add texture to your walls with cladding or funky wallpaper, or give plain walls a simple makeover with faux panelling (page 122).

I have the hardest time finding lights that I adore, so oftentimes I make my own: the letter light (page 142), and cute jelly mould light (page 108) are great projects to start with.

My number one budget saving tool and best friend – without question – is paint. Fresh paint can transform a space or a piece of old furniture, so it helps to understand the different types of finish on offer, and the amazing effects you have to play with (page 116).

This chapter is packed with practical tips and ingenious ways to get creative. It's all easy stuff that will enhance your interior, boost your mood and make you rethink the space you're in. It's called decorating on a shoestring, and I love it!

Paint Finishes

Once you understand the differences in paint finish, you can mix and match to create impact and texture within a scheme.

Traditionally, you have a choice between *oil- and water-based paints.* Oil-based paints are being phased out of the market due to their high VOCs (volatile organic compounds), which contribute to pollution. But they are still in demand, as they give great depth of colour, intense gloss and a durable finish. Water-based paints emit very little odour, dry quickly and are friendly to the environment, but they are not so great on demanding surfaces such as doors, furniture and floors.

In terms of finish, the accepted wisdom is to opt for a *matte or silk emulsion* for walls and ceilings, complemented by an eggshell or gloss for woodwork and trim. But I've seen some cool apartments with glossy ceilings, walls and floors, so it totally and utterly depends on the vibe you want to create!

Matte paint is the least reflective sheen available and gives a beautiful velvety finish. But for high traffic areas – kitchens, bathrooms, hallways – silk emulsion is a must as it's easily wipeable. As it's more reflective it shows every blemish, so make sure your walls are in good nick before applying!

Eggshell and satin paint have more of a sheen, giving well-plastered walls a lustrous look. I love the subtle effect you get with eggshell, where walls and woodwork gently merge into each other and you can't tell at a glance the difference in finish.

It goes without saying that all bare surfaces need a *primer* first, followed by an *undercoat* (page 182). And without trying to sound too preachy, I would strongly advise that you opt for a really good topcoat (my favourite brands are listed on page 188).

High quality paint is easier to apply, requires fewer coats, lasts longer and holds colour better. With bright colours, or the sludgies that I favour, the depth of pigment is noticeably superior due to the high quality ingredients used.

Top Tip

If you want to cut down on costs, simply undercoat in a cheaper paint that approximates the colour of the topcoat – it will cut your budget by half!

Paint Effects

This is where the fun starts! There are zillions of ways to create effects, from dragging, sponging, antiquing, marbling, verdigris, faux leather, block printing, faux bois and trompe l'oeil. You can add as much interest and texture to your walls as you like.

• *Faux bois* replicates the appearance of wood and, despite having been around since the late 19th century, it's suddenly everywhere. To do it yourself, you need two contrasting paints from the same colour family (see right), plus a wood-graining tool. Simply paint the light colour first, wait for it to dry; thin the darker colour with a 3 to 1 water to paint ratio and drag the graining tool through the still wet paint. Vary the direction of the tool to up the decorative interest.

• *Marbling* is fabulous and super easy. Sand down and prep your surface and decide on your colour palette: you will

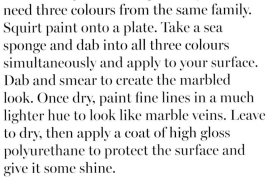

need three colours from the same family. Squirt paint onto a plate. Take a sea sponge and dab into all three colours simultaneously and apply to your surface. Dab and smear to create the marbled look. Once dry, paint fine lines in a much lighter hue to look like marble veins. Leave to dry, then apply a coat of high gloss polyurethane to protect the surface and give it some shine.

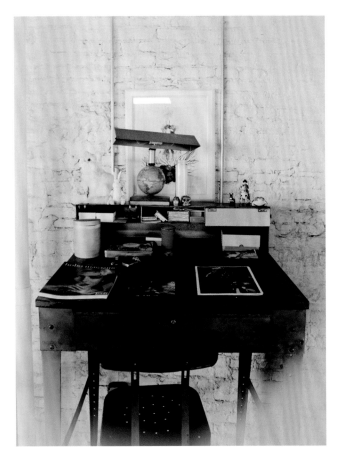

• *Dragging* is a really versatile painting technique. It's not unlike wood graining, in that you're dragging the paint bristles through wet paint, but the emphasis is on choosing striking colour combos to add rich layers of colour and texture to walls.

how to transform an old canvas *Banksy style*

Every house needs an injection of tongue-in-cheek style, and I am the hugest fan of buying cheap flea market art and scrawling over it in a shocking hue. First up, it adds an instant rock 'n' roll vibe and secondly it costs next to nothing. This idea is inspired by Bansky, who scrawled graffiti-style text onto a landscape hanging over Kate Moss's fireplace. For this version, I picked up an old sign at a flea market, fell in love with the rust and then scrawled on it in hot pink.

1. Practise your graffiti on a piece of card the same size as your painting/old canvas.

2. It's as simple as figuring our your phrase and painting it on. I'd say you want more paint on the brush than you would normally opt for, in order for the writing to really stand out.

Top Tip

Make your text standout by painting it in an amazing high voltage colour.

SHOPPING LIST

- Cheap landscape/ old canvas
- Card for practising
- Paint brush
- Artists' paint (acrylic or oil-based, depending on the effect you're after)
- White spirit to clean the brush, if opting for oil-based paint

Statement Decorating
A coffee table crafted from old
wood, Ikea slip covers skimming
a sofa, vintage taxidermy, flea
market mirrors and accessories.
This is called decorating with
panache. Style has absolutely
nothing to do with money and
everything to do with how a room
makes you feel. This one: squishy,
happy, relaxed!

Fyi The more layers you add
to a room the more interesting
it becomes. Case in point, this
beautiful bedroom. Throws
over throws, rugs hanging from
walls, a spray painted chair.
All brought together with the
softest palest summer cloud
grey on the walls; the perfect
hue for chilling out.

Wonderful Walls

One of the easiest ways to add personality to your space is by embellishing your walls. In fact, the secret to having one of the coolest designed pads in town is actually the wall detailing. Cover your walls in some fabulous wallpaper, panel them with floorboards, or simply display personal quirky collections, from artwork to letters to clothes. I've got great big moose heads scattered all over my walls, as well as an oddball collection of art. The more ad hoc you can be with your groupings the better – informal arrangements create a totally laid-back vibe. It's all about adding decorative layers to create a fab home gallery!

A Decorative Layer

Cladding or covering walls in unusual ways brings zing to your pad. With wooden panelling on the walls, the texture and patina are beautiful enough to need only the simplest decorating. If you have plain walls, consider adding art for an edgy twist.

how to
faux
panel

Top Tip

Paint the panelling out
in a contrasting hue
to your wall colour for
maximum impact.

SHOPPING LIST

- Spirit level
- Long ruler
- Tape measure
- Masking tape
- Pencil or chalk
- Paint
- Small paint brush

Give rooms a simple makeover by painting plain walls lacking any sort of architectural interest or distinction with faux mouldings. This is high impact stuff, takes no time at all, and makes any wall feel far grander than it really is.

1. Draw the frame: start by choosing where you want the top line of your panel perimeter. Use the spirit level and the ruler to mark a straight line. Measure the thickness you like (I used 2cm) and create a second line below the first.

2. Using the same method, draw a vertical line from the outer edge of the top line down to the length you like. Use the spirit level again to make sure it is straight. Measure the same thickness as the top line (2cm) and mark a second line inside the first. Do this again for the other side. When both 'frame' sides are drawn, connect the two outer lines at the bottom and measure the same thickness again to complete the frame. You may find a tape measure helpful to keep a check on the measurements throughout.

3. Tape just outside the frame lines using the masking tape. Make sure it is pressed down firmly.

4. Depending on the colour of the wall beneath, paint two to three coats to get a strong, standout effect.

5. When the paint is dry, remove the painter's tape in the direction of the fresh paint.

6. Looking for a little something extra? Try hanging an eye-catching print in your new 'gallery' space.

Idiosyncrasy Animal accessories add a sense of the unexpected to one of the most practical spaces in the house.

Be fearless when it comes to mixing materials.

Friction Mix wood with concrete, glass with steel – the more unconventional materials you combine, the more exciting your space.

Space Storage doesn't have to be dull. Wall-mounted racks free up cabinet space and give this most utilitarian space a stylish edge.

Concrete Walls, counters and floors look super sophisticated when skimmed in this simplest of materials.

Room Analysis

Embellishing furniture

Nobody wants their pad to look like it's been decorated by numbers, everything from the same recognisable sources. Embrace individuality. With a few tricks, it's easy to make high street and flea market finds uniquely your own.

- Paint drab, vintage pieces with blackboard paint and get creative with chalks for a jaw on the floor look (page 138).

- Take vintage chairs and tables to the garage for a cheap spray job that looks like the finest lacquer. I do this all the time – the results are tantalising!

- Transform smaller pieces yourself with a spray can and some PlastiKote spray paint – it's wondrous stuff, with finishes from faux stone to metallic.

- Spray an old vase, urn or classic furniture gold or silver. It's like adding jewellery to an outfit – every space needs a bit of bling!

- Mismatch. In Paris recently, I saw an amazing table with each leg painted out in a different hue. A cinch to do yourself, and such a fab way to make something look and feel gorgeously bespoke.

- Discover découpage (page 132), or use masking tape and bright paint to give a plain piece of furniture sensational stripes.

- If you're going to the trouble of getting something professionally done, upholster in a print or colour that shouts "Look at me!"

Handle Change One of the easiest ways to embellish featureless cupboards, drawers, dressers and consoles is by changing the handles. For a cheap fix, try spray painting existing handles in vibrant colours or paint out. Embellish handles with fabric. Or visit any hardware store for a quirky range of knobs and handles.

"I am a little obsessed with embellishing furniture. It's addictive stuff – you'll never look at flea market finds in the same way again!"

Top Tip

Work out which parts of the furniture are going to be covered with paper and measure them. If you're not sure, use scraps of newspaper based on these measurements to ensure everything fits well, before you start cutting into your best paper.

how to découpage a table

SHOPPING LIST

- Sandpaper
- Damp cloth
- Old magazines
- Découpage glue
- Paint brushes
- Clear varnish (suitable for wallpapered and painted surfaces)

Découpage is a fun way to make something boring look totally unique. It's also simple, cheap and can be applied to any plain old furniture. The trick here is to seek out unusual images. I découpage with old vintage comics, maps or labels. I find the colour palette softer and the piece always looks and feels more expensive than it really is.

1. Sand down the surface of your furniture, then wipe with a damp cloth to remove any debris.

2. Tear the magazine pages into lots of small pieces. Don't cut them, as you'll want the rough edges for a decorative effect.

3. Brush the glue onto the surface of the furniture.

4. Paste the scraps over the furniture in a random pattern. Use your fingers or the palm of your hand to gently smooth the paper over and stick it down.

5. Paint one more layer of glue over the top to seal the scraps. Be sure to let each coat dry completely before you do the next.

6. When dry, coat with a clear varnish to protect it from scratches and spills.

Savvy Storage

Fail to maximise your storage and you'll end up with a mess. Nail it and your life will become a million times easier, with everything running efficiently and comfortably at last.

The key with storage is to use all the empty, unused space available. Invest in multi-purpose furniture. Add rails, hooks or shelves to the insides of doors and cabinets. Bedrooms, kitchens and bathrooms are all key storage areas: if you can, build the storage units to the ceiling, paint them out the same colour as your walls, enhancing the impression of space.

Utilise your hallway – it's got massive storage potential, plus a hallway devoid of clutter makes an orderly impression! In my house, a super skinny console holds keys, leads and bus passes and the walls are accessorised with cool hooks for bags and coats. Shoes piled up by the front door are a no no by the way: try a low slung shelf painted out the same colour as the wall.

It's all about getting organised and being inventive with the details: I plop sunglasses on top of old busts. I use little hand-thrown bowls for storing loose change and keys. When I run out of cupboard space I utilise old hat boxes, which look sweet atop a shelf or wardrobe. Log baskets break up the formality of a space, and are also great for holding magazines, newspapers and a stash of unread paperbacks.

A Sense of Drama

Paint everything the same colour and immediately you've upped the style ratings. These standard Ikea shelves almost recede from view, making the accessories on display look and feel super glamorous. Add a twist: the outsized clock in here gives the room a big fat exclamation point, and elevates the whole look.

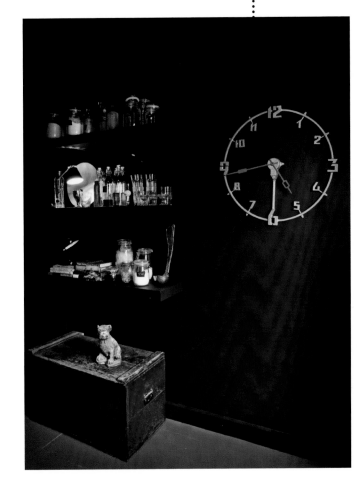

Make it Personal

Anything ugly looking goes behind closed doors, but show off the things you love. Open displays add personality to a space.

Volumes of Style

Some pieces are meant to be displayed, which is where open storage comes in. From pictures to objects to candles to letters, it's all about offering up interesting and diverse arrangements to add personality to a space.

If you have tons of books, put some thought into how you arrange your volumes on the shelf. Plonk objects in front, on top; intersperse books with pictures, beloved ornaments, stuff!

A mini library makes a great focal point in a room. But throughout my house there are also piles of books on coffee tables, occasional tables, by the bedside, on the kitchen island, even in the loo. I am a big fan of books being part of one's tablescape (as the Americans call it), as they make a lovely personal statement and add great shots of colour. Pile them in a higgledy-piggledy fashion – horizontally, vertically, at any angle – plonk a candle or a little bunch of blooms on top, and you've created the sweetest vignette.

Create More Space
Be sure your kitchen has style and character by making the most of the space you have available, floor to ceiling. Shelves and hooks maximise space, and there's even room for a mini bar! Open storage like this means you avoid dominating wall units.

Any Neglected Nook
can be used as office space. Take this NYC apartment where space is at a premium. A streamlined desk blends effortlessly with the furnishings; by accessorising it with non-officey stuff like lamps, art and a cool chair it looks sleek, stylish and in tune with the overall scheme. Genius!

how to chalkboard furniture

SHOPPING LIST
- Sandpaper (fine to medium)
- Blackboard paint
- Paint brushes
- Chalk

Chalkboard paint is another finish I am a little bit in love with. Simply take any not-so-nice piece of furniture you have lying around and paint it out. It will look amazing once you've scrawled over it in chalk. Super gallery-esq!

1. Prepare the piece of furniture by giving it a light sanding down.

2. Paint with blackboard paint; this will typically require at least three coats for a smooth, opaque finish.

3. When fully dry, let your imagination go wild with a bit of chalk.

Top Tip

When accessorising a piece such as this console, restrict the colour palette of the things going on top (the vases, artwork, lights and so on) to ensure the focus is on the statement furniture.

Back to Brown Brown furniture is one of the cheapest, easiest things to pick up second-hand. The trick to making it look glamorous rather than granny-ish is in the styling. Here a restricted colour palette, and plants, pots and tubs of varying heights provide visual intrigue. And the jewellery hung from a cheap coat hook is a genius idea: first, it adds an interesting layer to the walls and second, it's super practical. Brown furniture just got way cooler!

Crazy or Cool?
Bookcases crafted from old planks of wood; a vintage flag suspended between windows; the odd grandma armchair and floor lamp. Sounds crazy, but it works because the overall tone is unified, leaving it to one or two colours to elevate the look.

how to
make your own
letter lights

I'm obsessed with fonts and typography letters in particular. They are very expensive to buy, even at flea markets, so I decided to make my very own, taking it a step further and making a carousel light.

1. Select a font you like and then print a letter as large as you can. If you want to supersize your letter you can always get it printed out at a copy centre.

2. Cut the letter out of the paper, then put the cutout on the foam board and using the scalpel, follow the lines to cut the letter out. You can use your ruler to help with straight lines.

3. Figure out where you are putting your lights. You will want to space them out evenly, and the gaps you leave will vary based on the size of your bulbs. Make an indentation with the scalpel and then enlarge it by using a marker pen or pencil (depending upon the size of your bulbs).

4. Insert the bulbs through the back of the foam board.

5. Cut a strip of matte board to fit each side of the letter. The width of your cut will create the depth of the letter, so do what you like and what fits best based on the size of the foam board cutout.

6. Attach the sides to the interior using the hot glue gun: run a length of glue along the edges of the foam board letter, then attach the sides. You will want the strips to overlap the foam board on both sides.

SHOPPING LIST
- Printed out letter
- Scissors
- 5mm black foam core board (for the interior)
- Cutting mat
- Scalpel
- Ruler
- Fairy lights
- Marker pen or pencil
- 5mm black matte board (for the sides)
- Hot glue gun

Top Tip

Opt for fairy lights rather than LED lights; they make a far cooler decorative statement.

The details

I often think that people stop decorating too soon. Quite rightly we concern ourselves with the practical stuff first. But the devil, as they say, is in the detail.

Home accessories are the stuff that turn a pad from mundane to magical in a nanosecond. Decorative statements add layers, and the more layers you pile on, the better.

Don't worry about mixing everything up – add a giant lamp, oodles of rugs skimming the floor, a salon style art wall (page 172); throw in the odd kitsch figurine, inject warmth with cushions, books, vases, mirrors, flowers, scent – all those things that make your heart skip a beat the moment you walk through the door.

The trick, as ever, is to rein in the colour palette and then you can combine baroque style vases with sleek mirrors, or funny little sketches with classic ornaments – there really are no limitations.

Personal keepsakes give a room soul and make it intriguing, but there is a knack to displaying your favourite curiosities. Tableaux don't just happen, they get worked on, tweaked, perfected so as to look like they've just been thrown together (page 157).

This chapter will show you how to accessorise with attitude and inject instant personality into a room with carefully curated collections. It's all about the details: the more you add the more interesting your space will become!

Lighting

If you happen to have just one pendant hanging from the ceiling, please do something about it – I am thinking about campaigning to make this a criminal offence! Lighting should never be an afterthought in a decorating scheme but part of your plan from the early stages. You need three types for happy living. Ambient or general background lighting; task lighting for working, reading and cooking; and accent lighting to add depth and shade, and decorate an area.

Layering is my top tip for any lighting scheme – so mix and match with aplomb a selection of pendants, floor, table and recessed lights, not to mention a smattering of candles and delicate fairy lights for added intrigue. There is a common misconception that you have to light the whole room. But what we are after are soft pools of light coming from a variety of sources, tantalising the eye with highlights and lowlights.

Dimmers allow you to play about with a gamut of tones, from soft to dazzling, for day or night.

Floor Lights add a vertical dimension to a room and bounce the light around at different levels.

Overhead Lights should not be the main source of illumination as they cast a rather flat, dull light and unflattering shadows. Think of them instead as co-conspirators.

Supersized Lights give a space that Alice in Wonderland feel. Even tiny rooms can take one.

Table Lights radiate light inwards and cosy a space up.

Wall Lights are fab for washing walls with beautiful tones.

Light Fantastic

The more lights you have in a space the more magical it will become. My rooms are fairly small and I have at least seven different lights glowing away in each. When the lighting is warm, diffused and layered, you hardly notice it; a space simply feels comfortable and relaxed. Get it wrong and no one wants to linger, me included!

A Shadowy Art

Shadow adds depth to a room, so don't try to eliminate it. Instead, I always opt for a softer wattage bulb so everything below is washed a little more gently.

Room Analysis

Space Open plan kitchens should harmonise with the rest of your space. A unifying style and paint colour will help when transitioning from one area to the next.

Lights Hang a chandelier above the kitchen island, pop a supersized table lamp on the worktop. This is the social hub of your home, so don't waste the opportunity to dazzle!

Layers Take a kitchen from utilitarian to glamorous by adding candles, vases and decorative objects.

Display Clearing worktops of rarely used kitchen gadgets opens up space for a display of favourite recipe books or some big blousy blooms.

Give your kitchen as much respect as your living room.

Statement Lighting

In any interior, I always want one of my lights to make a statement that stops people in their tracks. Anything supersized looks amazing. Ditto anything uber glam, sparkly or in wondrous hot shades. Whatever the fixture, an element of quirk or whimsy goes a long way. It's all about balance and control, so think of pairing over-sized shades with discreet wall-mounted fittings, or delicate floor lamps with flamboyant table lights. If your lighting scheme can create a vibrant mood and pack a visual punch as well, then you've pretty much nailed it!

Top Tip

Table lights are one of my best friends when it comes to decorating. Not only do they help set the mood, they radiate light inwards making a space feel uber cosy. They are a great starting point for styling a table, a console or even a mantle. Furniture is mostly horizontal so, with their strong verticals, they break up a room magnificently.

Display

Accessories are a wonderful form of self-expression and the easiest way to inject colour, pattern and texture into a room. Think about all the different things you treasure – prints, sculptures, figurines, magazines, paperweights, bookends, vases, plates – and figure out what might look good together.

● Don't worry about leaving space between objects – too contrived. Instead, vary the heights of your display items.

● Stick to two or three main colours.

● Cluster by shared colour, tone, material or shape, so that no matter how diverse the objects are in other ways they immediately make visual sense and your display feels curated.

● Don't line your accessories up. Layer. We want 3-D displays that are beautiful, eclectic and never stuffy.

● Pay attention to scale. If you can't see a small object clearly, from the other side of the room, ditch it.

● Don't be afraid to mix eras, styles, textures and patterns. In fact the more you mix the more enticing your display will be.

Trial and Error
Tableaux don't just happen, they get worked on, tweaked, perfected. Try out different arrangements to see what looks best.

Forget Symmetry
Balance is important, symmetry is not. You don't want to match too much, neither do you want one end of your shelf or table covered with objects and the other end empty. It will feel like a sinking ship!

Accessorising with Attitude

For me, the most successful interiors always have an element of the unexpected – something wacky or whimsical, kitsch, haphazard or goofy that adds a vital dose of fun to a space and stops it from becoming too serious.

My rule of thumb: between 80 and 90 per cent of a space should be well-coordinated, harmonious, balanced, la la la. But then the remaining 10 to 20 per cent should be a little off the wall and bursting with personality!

In my pad I've got papier-mâché elephants hanging out on mantles, dog lights sitting on ostrich tables, big plaster birds on consoles. I've plonked sunglasses on old busts, sat an old gnome from an amusement park on my balcony, and put a seriously bad piece of art on my bedroom mantelpiece. They all add that tongue-in-cheek twist that makes me smile when I enter a room!

Lighten Up! You need one or two pieces that are going to envelope you with warmth and make you laugh, otherwise it can all feel a little

Curated Curiosities

Accessorising with attitude doesn't have to be totally oddball. You might collect cameras, musical instruments, figurines or art. The idea is to display the stuff you love, instead of hiding it away. If you gather and cluster your collections into groups, they become a focal point in the room. What's more, they will give you that feeling of squishy contentment I get every time I come home. It's easily achieved if you surround yourself with stuff you love!

Going Mini Gotta love a mini bar! For a cool boutique hotel vibe, accessorise with lamps, flowers and some background art. Then pull the look together by plonking everything on a sturdy tray.

how to make a thrifty designer vase

SHOPPING LIST
- Glass vase
- White spirit
- Cloth
- PlastiKote textured spray paint

One of my favourite quick revamps is to spray cheap glass vases with textured paint to make them look and feel more expensive than they really are. I'm a big fan of the PlastiKote stone finish but you can go metallic, glossy, aluminum, gold or silver, depending on the effect you're after. Simply pop some delicate blooms in there and wait for the compliments to come flooding in!

1. Thoroughly clean the surface of your vase with white spirit and a damp cloth.

2. In a well-ventilated area, carefully spray-paint the outside of your vase in a smooth, even manner. The trick is to spray quickly and evenly in all directions, moving the can from side to side and up and down.

Top Tip

You need a well-ventilated area so I always opt for outside, and practise spraying on a piece of newspaper first.

Flower Power

With their colour palettes changing with the seasons, flowers perk up the most boring of displays. Pop a few dahlias in a marmalade pot or some hand-tied blooms in jam jars and suddenly you've transformed a little nook into something sweet and dreamy.

I've learnt a few tricks from having a sister as a florist, like cutting the stems off flowers so their heads just peak and topple over vases (so elegant), or sprinkling red roses with glitter for some added sparkle at a dinner party.

Don't be afraid to fake it. I've been obsessed with faux blooms ever since I discovered some amazing ones in Holland, which I now sell, and they've transformed my interiors! I opt for big blousy varieties, English in feel – hydrangeas, English tea roses, fat-headed dahlias. And I alternate with the seasons.

Flowers fresh or faux really are the five minute face-lifts of the decorating world. I find them irresistible!

Fuse with Aplomb   Our homes should reveal something about who we are and what we like; they should provide an interesting range of ideas. Be fearless in your decorating choices. With a mix of high, low, vintage and high street, your home will tell a story other people want to listen to and hang out in!

"You can't get this look from one store, whether that's a chain like Ikea or a designer like Ralph Lauren."

Lifting a Space Out of the Mundane

Accessorising with attitude is all about pushing the envelope. Decorating like this requires no formal training, no complicated understanding of the principles of design. The trick? Simply buy something that makes you smile. It could be as simple as flea market art in odd frames; or displaying a seriously large light on a table that is too small. The important thing is that you are delightfully thinking out of the box. Have fun with it!

Candles make a beautiful statement, from a quirky candle holder to a smattering of tea lights to large hurricane vases as centrepieces. I have a series of hand hooks, similar to the one shown left, all over my walls. It's a modern take on a wall sconce and there is something magical about positioning candles close to walls. I also group a series of mismatched candles on my mantelpiece around mirrors to reflect the light. When dusk falls, it's beautiful. And their flickering, flattering light creates magic at night!

Art

One of the easiest ways to inject personality into a room is through the stuff you hang on your walls, be that contemporary paintings, framed book covers, flea market finds or old family snaps. I'm forever hanging prints or artwork that I've bought abroad, along with the odd holiday snap – it's a great way of documenting your life. Art is a real conversation starter; it has a back story and brings a space alive. One rule: if you don't 100 per cent love it, don't buy it!

Salon Style One of the hot trends of the moment is to display your artwork salon style – higgledy-piggledy in other words.

Hang in There

If you have a mixed bag of art, or if your art doesn't warrant hanging on its own, then a salon style art wall is a fabulous option. When looking at the wall, the eye is drawn to the installation as a whole, rather than concentrating on one or two cheap finds, and you can get creative with the composition.

For me, the most important thing to remember when it comes to arranging art is that there is no specific formula. Don't get hung up about making sure everything is perfectly aligned. Mix drawings with photos, watercolours with letters, oils with magazine tears. In fact, the best advice I can offer is not to overthink it – just enjoy the process!

Top Tip

It's not just about the art, the frame is important too. Mix and match modern with traditional, metal with distressed gold. It all helps up the visual interest.

Personal Displays Walls are a great way of telling a story about who you are, your travels and experiences. Hang as you like. And maybe save a few pieces to lean or prop against a wall, shelf or mantelpiece to create a totally laid-back vibe.

Composition

Before displaying your artwork on the walls you may want to try a few layouts on the floor. You can than either cut a template the size of each picture and play around with it on the walls or use painters' tape to outline each picture to help you visualise the installation on the blank walls. You need an anchor or focal point to start, so select one picture from which to build. This doesn't have to be centred. In fact, for an easy bohemian vibe, it's best if you don't start in the centre. Once you're happy with the design, start hammering. Alternatively you can do as I do. Forget templates and plans and just start hammering!

A Fine Art If you're hanging just one picture or a little row of pictures, for example, be sure to hang at eye level. Too high or too low and the wall will look odd and unbalanced.

Practical stuff

Five golden rules

I've packed this book with plenty of practical tips and quick revamps to help you decorate on a shoestring budget. If you're a DIY novice, embarking on a decorating project can feel scary. But there are so many positives to doing it yourself, like saving money and gaining a ton of confidence and satisfaction along the way. Just follow my five golden rules:

1. Have patience. I literally have none, but experience has taught me not to rush a job. Take time and you can carry anything out with aplomb.

2. Figure out what you need before embarking on a project. Sounds obvious, but planning is vital, so make sure you have the correct tools for each step of a job.

3. Make sure you have enough space to work in.

4. Make sure that whatever you are working on is properly prepped, cleaned and ready to go.

5. If it's your first project don't try and be overly ambitious – it will put you off. Start small and work your way up.

The Essential Tool Kit

It may not look very comprehensive but this simple kit is all that's required to undertake the majority of the projects in this book. Forget heaps of tools that get used infrequently and instead keep it to a minimum – it feels less scary that way.

- Cutting knife
- Cutting mat
- Electric drill with hole cutter
- Glue gun
- Hammer
- Masking tape
- Metal ruler
- Paint
- Paint brushes (natural bristle are best)
- Pencil
- Phillips screwdriver
- Picture hooks
- Pincers
- PlastiKote
- Retractable tape measure
- Ruler
- Scissors
- Sugar soap
- White spirit

Painting Tips and Techniques

Preparing Your Surfaces

Chemical method Ready-made solutions for stripping paint and varnish come in tins, aerosols or spray bottles and most are water washable. If applying from a tin, use an old but good-quality brush to spread the liquid thickly and evenly in one direction over the surface. Leave for the recommended time (normally 20–30 minutes). Remove loose paint with a broad paint scraper, steel wool or old rags – stubborn spots may require a second coat of remover. Always wear chemical-resistant gloves and a face mask when applying.

Heat method Apply a hot-air gun or blowtorch to painted surfaces, keeping it moving to avoid scorching the wood. (You can remove any slight marks by rubbing down with fine sandpaper.) Scrape away the paint as soon as it blisters and peels. Do not use near glass as the heat can cause it to crack. Wear gloves, a face mask and safety goggles.

Sanding Removing paint with sandpaper alone is time consuming and inefficient; in addition, it is easy to spoil the surface of the wood underneath. Use coarse sandpaper, as the finer grades will clog up quickly. For a finer finish, use one of the preceding methods. Wear a face mask to avoid inhaling dust.

Filling a Hole or Crack

Surfaces such as walls, floors and woodwork should have any chips, cracks or holes filled before you decorate them. Wood filler is ideally suited to filling small to medium holes in wood – choose a colour to match the timber. An all-purpose filler is fine for walls and both this and wood filler are easy to apply, drying quickly ready for painting. A filler such as caulk can be applied with a gun, and so is useful for larger projects. Dislodge any loose material and apply the filler to the crack or hole with a broad filling knife. Wipe away any excess and then smooth the surface over with the blade. Sand when dry for a smooth finish and wash the wall with sugar soap. For deep holes, apply filler in layers, waiting for each to dry before applying the next.

Priming Wood

New wood should be sanded down lightly to smooth the grain and then sugar soaped. Brush knotting solution over bare knots to stop sap leaking out and spoiling the finished paintwork. Follow with a coat of wood primer.

Priming Walls

Primer is specially formulated to seal surfaces making sure paint adheres properly and creating a professional-looking finish. It is a good base coat and, used with an undercoat, may prevent the need to apply two or more coats of your more costly chosen paint. Make sure the wall or floor surface is clean and dry, with any holes and cracks filled. Apply as you would a topcoat with a roller or paint brush.

Undercoat

Undercoat is a thick paint which provides good, solid cover for a topcoat. On bare or new surfaces use a primer first. Surfaces that have been painted before need only an undercoat. Remember: an undercoat is always a primer (it provides a smooth, even surface for topcoats); but a primer is not an undercoat – think of it as a base or first coat. An undercoat is particularly useful if the existing shade of paint is darker than the one you intend to apply. Choose one that matches the shade of your topcoat and apply with a roller or paint brush.

Sanding by Hand

All wood should be sanded before painting in order to achieve the best finish. Sandpaper is available in different degrees of coarseness, known as grades. The lower the number, the coarser the grade. Most timber should be sanded with medium-grade (120–150) and then finished off with fine (180–220). You also need to lightly sand between coats of paint to provide a 'key' for the next layer. After sanding, surfaces should be sugar soaped and then wiped clean of debris with a lint-free cloth and white spirit.

Calculating What You Need

How much paint you need depends on the size and nature of the surface you are painting. On average, you can reckon on a coverage of 10 square metres per litre of paint. For rougher surfaces halve this. Most surfaces will require more than one coat to ensure good coverage. A tin of paint will always need a stir before you use it to ensure that all its elements (pigment, oil) are well combined for a more even coat and finish. A simple stick will do the job so long as it reaches the bottom of the paint tin.

The Paint Job

Rollers, brushing and spraying are our choices when it comes to applying paint, each creating their own effect.

Rollers are easy to use and to clean. They make the job faster, especially over large surfaces, but create more splattery mess. You will still need a brush at the joins with the ceiling and door, and the finish will have a slight 'orange peel' appearance.

Brushes give you great control, make less mess and are essential for a fine application of paint in hard-to-reach places. Quality paint brushes make a huge difference to the end result. Think of them as you do make-up brushes and go with natural bristles, which hold the paint much better than synthetic ones and are also much more flexible, enabling a smoother application.

Spraying gives a fine professional finish but stick to small items such as pieces of furniture and picture frames. It's a messy business and so is best done outdoors. To get a finish that looks expensive I go to a car spray-painter to spray my furniture.

Cleaning Up

Look after brushes and rollers – these should be cleaned immediately after use. First, remove excess paint with a paint stirrer or stick. If using a water-based product, clean the brush or roller thoroughly in soapy water (the roller sleeve should be removed first). White spirit will remove oil-based paint but don't leave brushes to stand on their bristles in solution for a long period of time as this will cause the brush to lose its shape. Work the white spirit or soapy water through the bristles to ensure all paint is removed. Shake off any excess liquid and dry with a lint-free cloth.

Looking After Yourself

DIY can be a mucky business, so wear overalls or set aside some old clothes especially for decorating – just make sure the sleeves and legs are not too loose and flappy or they could catch on things and become a safety hazard. Always make sure that your room is properly ventilated when working with oil-based paint and varnish to avoid inhaling strong fumes. Open doors and windows to allow a good supply of fresh air to flow through and to enable fumes to escape. Wear a face mask to increase protection.

Little Black Book

I spend a lot of time each year travelling for work – to NYC, Paris, Sydney and Melbourne, as well as around London of course – so many of my favourite addresses relate to these cities. Having said that, here's where you'll find one of the coolest stores on the planet in Milan, a bonkers-but-brilliant Dutch furniture shop, the UK's best out-of-town antique fairs, plus the most amazing online supplier of vintage wallpaper, and the cheapest designer taps on the high street. The shops are organised by style, but really there's something for everyone in most of these amazing stores, so go with an open mind and a clear vision of what you want.

CLASSIC

Astier de Villatte (France)
www.astierdevillatte.com
This chic Parisian store specialises in tableware. I love the hand-thrown ceramics. If I could, I would get married ten times over just to get their pieces on my list!

Debenhams (UK)
www.debenhams.com
Cool homeware at high street prices, from John Rocha to Ben de Lisi.

John Derian (USA)
www.johnderian.com
King of découpage, John Derian inspired the project I made on page 132. Trays, plates, paperweights are beautifully découpaged with vintage paper. His American stores sell textiles, lighting and furniture, either sourced globally or made under his own label.

Merci (France)
www.merci-merci.com
For me this Parisian haven is one of the most fabulous stores in the world.

Part used book café, part fashion house, part interiors emporium. The collection is beautifully curated; my jaw is on the floor every time I visit.

Ochre (UK)
www.ochre.net
A British based furniture, lighting and accessories design company, with a showroom open by appointment only in London and a store, selling beautiful hand-made sofas, armchairs and lighting, in a phenomenally beautiful building in Soho, NYC.

eclectic

ABC Carpet & Home (USA)
www.abchome.com
An Aladdin's cave of gorgeousness, this vast homeware store is full to the brim of stuff for the home, from tabletop to lighting to furniture, not to mention the rugs. You'll need a good hour or two to do it justice.

Anthropologie
www.anthropologie.com
With zillions of stores in the US and now four in the UK, Anthropologie is a great place to go for homeware. I can't get enough of their rugs, kitchen ware and one-off finds. Plus, check out how they merchandise and style the stores: lots of great inspiration to take home.

Caravan (UK)
www.caravanstyle.com
My friend, the author and stylist Emily Chalmers owns this fabulous shop in Old Spitalfields Market, offering a quirky selection of finds.

Michele Varian (USA)
www.michelevarian.com
I'm a big fan of this New York homeware designer. Great for decorative pillows, glassware, home accessories and a little quirk – at a wide range of prices.

Paul Smith (UK)

www.paulsmith.co.uk
I love Paul Smith's shop in Albemarle Street, London. It's expensive but it houses the most beautiful collection of unique antiques, objets d'art and curiosities, all with a Paul Smith twist.

Pure and General (Australia)

www.pureandgeneral.com
An eclectic collection of finds beautifully curated. The last time I visited I fell in love with the gorgeous Moroccan textiles and rugs.

Rossana Orlandi (Italy)

www.rossanaorlandi.com
Rossana's beautiful Milan shop is a visionary homeware store, right up there with Merci as one of the best in the world. Be sure to grab a coffee in her little café next door.

GLAMOROUS

Atelier Abigail Ahern (UK)

www.AtelierAbigailAhern.com
Possibly the coolest shop on the planet!! Can I say that about my own store? Hey ho, I just did.

Aston Mathews (UK)

www.astonmatthews.co.uk
Great for cool bathroom finds. If you want to up your style ratings at no extra cost, buy bath taps and install them over your sink. The effect is grander in scale, quirkier and way cooler; it's the thing I get quizzed on most when anyone visits my bathroom.

Comer & King (Australia)

www.comerandking.com
Cam Comer is an amazing interior designer who crafts some seriously cool textiles. His showroom is by appointment only, but don't let that put you off. With private commissions from all over the world, if you fancy something unique, he's your man!

Mint (UK)

www.mintshop.co.uk
A beautifully created collection of finds, often exclusive to Mint.

Nicole Farhi Home (UK)

www.nicolefarhi.com
Beautiful ceramics, furniture, textiles in the softest of palettes. Expensive but it lasts forever. I brought a big slubby throw from here fourteen years ago and it's still laying across my bed.

Second Hand Rose (USA)

www.secondhandrose.com
A totally fabulous vintage wallpaper source: the collection ranges from chinoisere to damask to faux finishes. And they ship all over the world.

ROCK 'N' ROLL

Jonathan Adler (USA)

www.jonathanadler.com
Jonathan Adler put humour into homeware Stateside with his happy, joyful accessories and furniture. I salute him!

Kühn Keramik (Germany)

www.kuehn-keramik.com
Ceramic art and pottery tableware that is edgy, tongue in cheek and totally ace.

Liberty (UK)

www.liberty.co.uk
Has a fabulous homeware section on the fourth floor, best in London for traditional and contemporary pieces, with a twist.

Moooi (Holland)

www.moooi.com
The collection of furniture, lighting and accessories is tongue-in-cheek, if not a little bonkers (life-size horses crafted from resin as a floor light, anyone?) Still, every home must have a dash of oddness to take it to another level and these guys will set you on your way!

Squint (UK)

www.squintlimited.com
Best known for her exuberant
patchwork designs, my friend Lisa
Whatmough, founder and owner of
Squint, has the most tantalising array
of furniture, accessories, lighting
and wallpaper. Everything is richly
decorative. I am the hugest fan.

BOHO

Baileys (UK)

www.baileyshomeandgarden.com
Much of the stock is vintage, including
some great lamps, and furniture that
has been restored, reworked and
brought to life. Shop online or at the
Bailey's home store in Ross-on-Wye,
Herefordshire.

Caravane (France)

www.caravane.fr
Beautiful textiles and homeware worth
checking out; there are a couple of
stores around Paris.

Doug up on Bourke (Australia)

www.douguponbourke.com.au
Industrial, rustic, laid-back – cool for
vintage finds, and how can you not
visit with a name like that?!

Ici et la (Australia)

www.icietla.com.au
Full to the brim with European finds,
from vibrant striped fabrics to zinc
letters to French garden furniture. It's
like stepping into a cool antiques store
in the heart of Paris except we are in
Australia. Amazing! Plus they have a
cool dog.

Izzi and Popo (Australia)

www.izziandpopo.com.au
A great selection of imported vintage
finds (mainly from Belgium markets).

Koskela (Australia)

www.koskela.com.au
Simple but well-crafted furniture and
accessories all made in Australia. (And
their latest store has a café that gets
incredible reviews in the press.)

Lassco (UK)

www.lassco.co.uk
A great resource for architectural
antiques, salvage and curiosities. I
brought huge wooden boards dragged
up from the River Stour for one of the
walls in my bedroom. Pricey, but truly
beautiful stuff.

Olde Good Things (USA)

www.ogtstore.com
Architectural items, altered antiques,
farm tables, industrial stuff and the
best vintage tin tiles on the planet
(believe me I've searched). They ship
all over the world and certainly on the
tile front nothing I've come across is
as good.

Saipua (USA)

www.saipua.com
The coolest florist in NYC (located in
Brooklyn): sells country-esque blooms
put together with absolute finesse.

The Old Cinema (UK)

www.theoldcinema.co.uk
Housed in a refurbished 1890s
cinema, this antiques, vintage and
retro store is a great resource for
vintage finds.

The Society Inc, Sibella Court (Australia)

www.thesocietyinc.com.au
Haberdashery, hardware and
super cool paint colours under the
Muroband label. It's teeny tiny and
off the beaten track, but well worth a
gander.

ANTIQUES

Alfies (UK)

alfiesantiques.com
This indoor market is one of the
coolest places to buy vintage in
London. Pretty pricey, but if you're
looking for that something special,
this is the way to go.

Atomic Antiques (UK)

www.atomica.me.uk
Atomic Antiques in east London has
a beautiful selection of vintage finds.
The owner has the best eye in town.

International Antiques & Collectors Fairs (UK)

www.iacf.co.uk/fairs
Europe's largest antiques and collectables events, held every other month. Out of town, but well worth the long haul. I mostly go to Ardingly and Newark. The trick is to go on trade day. You'll pay £20 to get in but come visitors' day (the day after) all the best stuff is gone.

Kempton (UK)

www.sunburyantiques.com
A twice monthly market (every other Tuesday) you will find me here most times, wrapped in the thickest of coats with pyjamas underneath in winter, since I need to get up at 4.30 a.m. to get there! And that's the key. Get there at the get-go, 6.30 a.m. with a torch, to find the bargains.

ONLINE BARGAINS

Gumtree & Preloved

www.gumtree.com
www.preloved.co.uk
Gumtree and Preloved were the two classified sites I most relied on when working on the TV programme, *Get Your House in Order*, for Channel 4. Most of the stuff listed is reasonable and you can shop by area to cut down the expense of getting stuff couriered across the country. I found dining tables, occasional tables and chairs from both of these sites.

Salvo (UK)

www.salvo.co.uk
You can buy anything from an old barn in Wales to a rustic old kitchen sink. A great resource for salvaged pieces, and the prices are not outlandish.

FLEA MARKETS

Les Puces de Saint-Ouen (France)

marcheauxpuces-saintouen.com
The most famous flea in Paris is the one at Porte de Clignancourt. Apparently it covers seven hectares, which is huge! In fact, it's the largest antiques market in the world, receiving up to 180,000 visitors each weekend. It's also expensive, so if you're looking for a bargain, this is not the place. Huge chandeliers from old country estates and some truly beautiful retro finds are all on display.

Porte de Vanves (France)

pucesdevanves.typepad.com
This weekend flea market near the Porte de Vanves metro stop is the oldest in Paris. Set among magnificent old plain trees, it's a heavenly place to visit and way less touristy than Clingnancourt. You have to barter; don't let the language put you off! I've come away with paintings, old leather chairs, dining chairs (which somehow I managed to smuggle back on Eurostar!) and a huge chandelier.

Brooklyn Flea (USA)

www.brooklynflea.com
Actually two flea markets, one in Fort Greene, NYC every Saturday (from April until November), the other in Williamsburg every Sunday. Fort Greene Flea is part vintage bazaar, part hipster hang out, with some amazing artisan food stalls. Williamsburg is smaller, but still great, especially on a day when the weather is fine and you can just zap across on the ferry from Manhattan. It's also worth pottering around the streets of Williamsburg to check out the indie stores that have set up home here.

The Antiques Garage, West 25th Street Market & Hell's Kitchen (USA)

www.hellskitchenfleamarket.com
If you're in NYC, these flea markets are a must-visit. The Antiques Garage has two large floors full of vintage fabrics, rugs, furniture, every type of fine silver item imaginable, and more. West 25th Street Market features up to 125 vendors selling antiques, collectibles and other types of vintage and mid-century modern items. And my favourite, Hell's Kitchen includes vendors from The Annex Flea Market, formerly located in Chelsea.

PAINT

I buy paint samples like other people buy shoes; nothing sets my heart a racing more than a new paint colour on the market! Here are my favourites from around the world. You won't be able to order pots of paint from international stockists, so order colour charts and samples. If you love the colour, have it matched and get painting!

Farrow & Ball
www.farrow-ball.com

Marston & Langiner
www.marston-and-langinger.com

Little Green Paint Company
www.littlegreene.com

Zoffany
www.zoffany.com

Paint Library
www.paintlibrary.co.uk

Papers and Paints
papers-paints.co.uk

Murobond (Australia)
www.murobond.com.au

Flamant (Belgium)
www.flamantpaint.com

Emery & Cie (Belgium)
www.emeryetcie.com

Ressources (France)
www.ressource-decoration.com

Ralph Lauren (USA)
www.ralphlaurenhome.com

Martha Stewart Living Paint (USA)
www.homedepot.com

STYLE GUIDES

Blogs, books, interiors magazines and travel provide me with tons of inspiration, fresh ideas and different points of view. Pull out, flag or pin images that you love, and start creating your own personal style board (page 14).

Interiors Blogs

brightbazaarblogspot.com
Young British blogger with a penchant for colour and a total disregard for beige. His daily postings are fun and exuberant and he highlights all the latest trends so you can keep abreast of what's going on.

www.dailyimprint.blogspot.co.uk
Natalie Walton interviews some of the world's leading creatives for her blog, highlights cool homes as well as the latest book releases. Her interviews are always insightful and inspirational.

www.designspongeonline.com
Design Sponge is great if you're looking for some inspirational DIY projects. If you fancy launching a business of your own, Grace Bonney's Biz Ladies makes for pretty cool reading, and her Before and Afters are inspirational.

www.desiretoinspire.net
A joint blog run by two interior design junkies, desiretoinspire offers a feast of ideas, very well presented.

www.fromtherightbank.com
A sweet blog/journal about design, with some personal stuff thrown in, lots of inspirational images, and a ton on travel.

roselandgreene.blogspot.co.uk
I like the images on this blog. Rather than just rehashing what's in the latest magazine the choice is considered and always interesting – from a cool pad in Paris to a loft in NYC.

www.saipua.blogspot.co.uk
The most amazing florist in NYC chronicles her blooms and her experiences. Funny, straight from the heart, and I can relate in so many ways to the trials and tribulations, the highs and lows of running a business.

www.sfgirlbybay.com
Bohemian modern style from San Francisco-based blogger, photographer, stylist and flea market queen. Kind if makes me want to up sticks and move to San Fran.

www.thedesignfiles.net
I like the cross section of topics covered, from homes to retail to food to craft, and I dip into it every week.

www.theinteriorsaddict.com
Interiors, style, and personality profiles from stylish Sydney-based Brit.

www.theselby.com
Hip photographer Todd Selby shoots interesting people in their personal spaces, in a very relaxed way. I adore the shots he did of my pad, not so long ago. Very natural, uber laid-back, he uses only natural daylight so in some cases the images he shoots almost look like paintings. Adore!

Pinterest
If you see anything you like online, Pinterest.com is a completely addictive site that you can use to create virtual mood and design boards. A cross between an image-sharing social network and a bookmarking tool, it works by organising, or 'pinning' images that you love – cool products, design ideas and inspiration – from anywhere on the web. Use it to bring all the elements of your style together. Create your own Pinterest boards, or follow other Pinterest users and 'repin' their pins too. Hours of fun!

Books, Books, Books
I read in a big old velvet and tweed armchair, snuggled right by the fireplace in my studio. I have a bird's eye view over the garden in the summer, and in the winter a fire burns in the grate, so I turn my chair inward towards the flickering flames. Also in the studio is a floor-to-ceiling bookcase so it's the perfect place to pick up any tome. Here are my favourite reads:

Colour by Nathalie Taverne and Anna Lambert (Terra Uitgeverij)

Decorate by Holly Becker and Joanna Copestick (Jacqui Small)

Domino by Deborah Needleman (Simon & Schuster)

Etcetera, Nomad & The Stylist's Guide to NYC, all by Silbella Court (Murdoch Books)

Home by Stafford Cliff (Quadrille)

Modern Glamour and Hue by Kelly Wearstler (Harper Collins)

My Prescription for Anti-Depressive Living by Jonathan Adler (Harper Collins)

Sense of Style, Colour & Space by Shannon Fricke (Murdoch Books)

The Selby is in Your Place by Todd Selby (Abrahms Books)

Vintage Flowers by Vic Brotherson (Kyle Books)

Interiors Magazines
I have a zillion back issues of magazines from all over the world. I love *Elle Decoration UK* and *Livingetc* (UK); *www.lonnymag.com* (bi-monthly online); *Belle, Inside Out, Real Living* and *Vogue Living Australia* (Australia); and *Casa Vogue* and *Elle Decor Italia* (Italy).

Travel
If ever I am in a conundrum over a colour scheme, or am feeling overwhelmed by all the stuff in my head, I like to walk and take inspiration from the city. Nice, Marrakech, Paris and Berlin are all amazing cities to me, but NYC is one big inspiration. The Ace Hotel (www.acehotel.com/newyork) in midtown has one of the greatest lobbies on the planet: dark, snug and cocooning – with a great creative vibe. The Highline (thehighline.org), a public park built on an old elevated railway on the west side of Manhattan, has the most awesome planting scheme, and a magical colour palette. And for books, interiors, art, photography and more, Assouline (www.assouline.com/new-york.html), situated on the mezzanine at the Plaza Hotel, is the bee's knees.

INDEX

Acknowledgements

Thank you firstly to Anne Furniss and Helen Lewis at Quadrille for giving me the opportunity to write a second book. To Zelda Turner, my editor, who turned my rather oddball ramblings into coherent sense. To Nicola Ellis for the fab design. To Graham Atkins-Hughes, my good bud and super doper photographer – the images in this book elevate it to a whole other level!

Thank you to my team, Ainslee, Rose, Sharona and Simon, for all your hard work and support, and a big shout out to Rose for assisting on the book.

This book would not have come together without the wonderful people who allowed us to photograph their amazing homes:

Doub Hanshaw, creative director of Free People (www.freepeople.com)

Shauna Alterio and Stephen Loidolt, design duo behind Something's Hiding in Here (www.somethingshidinginhere.com)

Jordon Blackmore and Andi Potamkin, owners of art gallery/hair salon Three Squares Studio (www.threesquaresstudio.com)

Creative director and style guru Angel Dormer

Jean Christophe Aumas, director of Parisian creative agency Voice Voilà (www.voicivoila.com)

My business partner Gemma Ahern and designer Russell Lewis.

On a personal note, thanks to Gem, my sister, right hand lady and dearest bud, and her partner Russ, a fabulous artist in his own right, who penned the beautiful illustrations for each chapter opener and has done more for the business than I can possibly thank him for. To little Lily their daughter, who can't read yet but when she can, I love you Lils!

To Holly, my younger sister, who I never see enough of (despite the fact you live less than 40 miles away), and her husband, the author Lee Rourke. I cannot wait to see what you do with your fab new pad! To my parents for believing in me and always being there. Love you more than words can say Mummy and Daddy. To Gillian and Alan for their faith and unrelenting support, love, love, love you. To Mungo and Maud, my kids – I should really say my dogs – who brighten each and every day with their shenanigans.

Finally, but most importantly, to you guys. To the thousands of you that read my blog, visit the store, come along to the Design School, send heart-warming tweets and message me on Facebook. I cannot tell you how much it all means to me. Without you guys there is no business, so thank you big time for your support. This book is for you!

Publisher's note

The author and publisher take no responsibility for any injury or loss arising from the procedures or materials described in this book. Materials, tools, skills and work areas vary greatly and are the responsibility of the reader. Follow the manufacturer's instructions and take the appropriate safety precautions.

Editorial director: Anne Furniss
Art director: Helen Lewis
Project editor: Zelda Turner
Designer: Nicola Ellis
Photography: Graham Atkins-Hughes
Production: Leonie Kellman, Vincent Smith

This edition first published in 2013 by Quadrille Publishing Limited
Alhambra House
27-31 Charing Cross Road
London WC2H OLS
www.quadrille.co.uk

Text ©2013 Abigail Ahern
Design and layout © 2013 Quadrille Publishing Limited
Photography © 2013 Graham Atkins-Hughes

A catalogue record for this book is available from the British Library.

ISBN: 978 184949 272 0

Printed and bound in China